Simply be- Spring

By

Sheila Keegan Groome

Simply be-Spring ©2013 by Sheila Keegan Groome

All rights reserved

Condition of sale

This book is sold subject to the condition that it shall not, by way of trade or otherwise, be lent, re-sold, hired out or otherwise circulated in any form or binding or cover other than that in which it is published and without a similar condition including this condition being imposed on the subsequent purchaser.

ISBN number 978-1-304-49745-1

FOREWORD

My life is a constant battle of chaos and creativity, accepting the simple things is something I frequently forget. I have no frills in my life, nor hidden maids or attendees but enough love to sink a battle ship. I hope that eventually we can all (including me) stop fighting life and start loving it.

When I began writing this book it was a series of thoughts that I jotted down to remind myself what life was all about as I rushed through it. Now years later though I have a better balance I still yearn for many things without knowing what I actually need. The good news is I will always get what I need, not always what I want!

Simply be-Spring is a journey of self-discovery as I wander through life passing the days of spring, delightfully shaking off the dark duvet of winter. There are things I want to do, those that I must do, and those that I am afraid to even contemplate. Come and walk with me through the days as I clamber over lego and laundry on my journey, slowly carving out my world with the beauty and natural simplicity we are all surrounded by.

The book is designed to just dip into or read through or maybe just take a thought a day. It is the first in a series of four covering the seasons. It helps me realise that we are all in this life together wherever and whoever we are-if only we could just simply be.

Sheila Keegan Groome

December 2013

My first sign of spring is when I open the curtains for the first time in the morning and the sun is slowly rising at 7.30am. The depressing bowls of clay on my doorstep sprout green shoots and my heart lifts as the darkness of winter gradually falls away….

FEBRUARY

February 1st

Waiting

I hate waiting. I love doing. I love being in the thick of it but once in a while I just have to wait. When I want some decorating done at home that I cannot do myself then I have to wait until someone else is available. Or when I give in notice for a job and have to work the time out or I am awaiting a new home, a new baby or even just simply the new series of a favourite television programme, I have to allow time to take its course.

Waiting can be so tedious when actually, I want it now. But I am reminded of the fishermen who when not at sea braving all for their craft, are on the shore tending their nets and preparing their boats. Patiently they wait for the weather to change.

The reality of life is that regularly we must wait. Nonetheless this is time we had better not waste, we must try to use that time to prepare, plan, relax and rejuvenate so that we may be ready to, in reality, enjoy the change or the experience when it comes. Otherwise we will get so wrapped up in the waiting that it will seem it never comes quick enough. Then we will not be in the best frame of mind to particularly enjoy the event that we are so looking forward to when at last it does come to us.

~

February 2nd

On Patience

This is generally tested for me in two places: in the office and at home.
The workplace. Well even if you work in a tiny office with almost nobody or a huge call centre, there is often someone who gets on your nerves. They may do all sorts of things that try your patience and you may feel very justified in your irritation towards them.
At home. Well the type of patience that is required is different. If you have children, then you either have much more patience than me or way more minders. Children are a beautiful sacred creation and also are our greatest test. They discard objects, forget things, don't finish things and really live from moment to moment. We are often caught up in our own agenda and lost in our wish for how life must be. Naturally, family can get in the way and so patience begins to fray. They suffer selective deafness, repetitive traits and they can certainly push us when in the mood.
I have noticed though that when I wait with patience before reacting in both environments then I don't react. I respond. When I react it is an automated reaction to the moment and what's just happened or not happened. If I wait those ten seconds or so then I respond after thinking first,

then, they, whether they be adult or child, don't necessarily get the result they are anticipating from me. Frequently, the situation improves and I can clap myself on the back for having just that little piece of patience.

~

February 3rd

Spring beckons-so plant sunflowers

It is a couple of years since I have grown sunflowers. Today I picked up a packet of seeds in our town and set about planting them. The seed is so tiny and the pot so miniature that I have twelve of them on our windowsill in our kitchen. In the next couple of weeks they will shoot up and when the frost passes I shall plant them outside.
It is a lovely creative feeling at this time of the year. Bulbs you planted last year or someone else planted years ago are creeping up out of the ground. Baby birds are being born, soon the first lambs will arrive and the world is waking up from a big sleep.
Even if you suppose you are no good at gardening, with sunflowers you just can't miss. They are very hardy and will grow and grow. The joy and colour they provide will last long through to the summer months and the creative feeling their planting and growing gives you lasts all year.

So try it, get your hands dirty. Plant some seeds, water and wait. I guarantee you won't be disappointed.

~

February 4th

Throw those bills away

I don't know what it is about. But either in a perfect filing system or in a chaotic box we as a people commonly keep old bills. I started keeping till receipts in case I needed to return something to a shop and ended up with a bag full of bread and milk receipts that I do not need!
I absolutely think that you should check and file your bank statements as the margin for error is huge. The bills however need to go. Keep the important ones for maybe a year or two but dump/shred the rest. It will free up loads of space in the house.
Now what to do instead? Firstly out you go to a fabric or an art shop or both. You need pretty ribbon and a fancy box. And yes, maybe you've guessed it. Get out any love letters, postcards, notes or precious, personal memories and give them a good home.
Tie them up with pieces of ribbon. It might be a nice birthday card you once received or just a postcard. It could be a letter from someone who is

no longer around. Whatever is precious to you put them carefully in the box and put the box somewhere private in your bedroom.

Next time you are feeling that no one particularly understands you, or you are feeling a little down, your beautiful box of memories will be there waiting for you. It is a great deal more inviting than a sales slip!

~

February 5th

Selling our souls

Even though the mornings are getting a little brighter and the evenings are stretching a small bit some of us still rise in darkness and return home at dusk or nightfall. Lots of people change their jobs around the New Year but for those of us who have not or feel we cannot, at this time of year we can feel like our jobs are a very large part of our lives. In the summer, the evenings stretch out before us, however now some of us by 8pm often long to be tucked inside on couches or even in our beds.

As teenagers and school leavers we had big opinions and huge ambitions for our lives and not all of us have realised them fully. We should not be too hard on ourselves however, as we all need a roof over our heads and bread on the table and not every job can offer that.

Occasionally, in the workplace we can be asked to do duties that do not feel right or that do not sit well with us. Other days it is just the boredom and monotony that gets to us. We can feel on these days like we are wasting away and selling our souls. In short not being true to who we are or what we believe in for ourselves.

Occasionally, a day or two away can cure this, at other times we need to contemplate a career or lifestyle change but more often than not it is a compromise.

What we have to do though, in any event, is to use our spare time to fulfil our inner joy even if we do not feel we can change careers. Making whatever is making us unhappy feel like a smaller part of our lives (or eliminating it completely) is the key and so making everything else bigger reduces or eliminates the feeling that we are selling our souls.

~

February 6th

Can you see it?

Whatever is niggling in the back of your mind, bring it out today and have a little look at it. It might be a deed that you did or something you never got to do. Allow yourself some quiet time today and have a little think. Whatever has been rattling around in your head these past few weeks can be casting a shadow on your day. Release it and let it be. Deal with it and it will be gone.

It may be something as simple as cleaning the fridge or something big like changing your life. Why not get it out and take a look? Otherwise it is there tugging at you while you are living your life. It becomes that something that you keep pushing away and never face. If so then you never feel truly content.

So be brave, go for it. Look at your niggling thoughts. See them for what they are and then move on.

~

February 7th

Keeping up for the Jones'

Whatever about keeping up with the Jones', keeping up for them is even worse. When we are trying to keep up with the Jones' we are buying objects to be the same as everyone else so we do not look or feel left out. We often do not even need or want these encumbrances.

Keeping up for the Jones' is even worse. It involves purchasing items that we can ill afford to compete with people that we do not even like and ending up owning objects we probably will not even necessarily need.

In past years, in our society the pressures to appear

to be riding on the crest of the wave were huge. Everyone was doing so well we were told. In actual fact, everyone was exhausted attempting to keep up with how prosperous they believed everybody else was.

So step off that treadmill for a day and look at what you want out of life. Forget what others have or have not and concentrate on creating your world on your terms but most significantly with your means. Stop worrying about what others will or may already think about you and put your efforts and thoughts into keeping up with who you are. Times are tough as we come out of a recession and wondering about other people's lives will not help our own.

~

February 8th

On anger

When we are angry with someone it is extraordinarily difficult not to tell them what we assume they have done to us. Nonetheless, to be effective in communicating our feelings we actually have to try to concentrate on how we perceive the circumstances. Not "you make me feel" but "I feel because". Then all we are doing is describing ourselves and not passing a judgement on anyone else.

Now, though I know this, I do tend to complain about how I am spoken to or the attitudes of people towards me. I need to work on remembering that the only person for whose behaviour I am responsible is I.

In the same way if someone close to you disgraces themselves. You are not them. You are an entirely distinct person. And you do not own them. All you can do is show the way; carry the torch by your own actions. If their actions upset you, tell them, but don't blame them. They in turn must work out their own lives for themselves.

It is normal to be angry when the occasion justifies it. We have to be careful, however, how we express our anger.

~

February 9th

Being spontaneous

It is hard to be spontaneous with a young family or a heavy workload. Indeed, habits are good in their own way. Everyone knows what to expect and feels secure in the routine. Sometimes despite this it is vital to be spontaneous. Spontaneity can be expressed by an extraordinarily simple act like dancing in the kitchen to the radio. Or skipping with your daughter's skipping rope. Or going out for a day out on a Saturday instead of whatever you usually do.

It is like the old saying "a change is as good as a rest". This time of year it is weeks until Easter and over a month to Paddy's Day so you need a little lift.

If you have children or are young at heart a run up a mountain and a picnic in winter coats at the top is a great hit. Or if you prefer something warmer make a picnic in your living room, rug and all, sit on the floor and eat. It will instantly relax you because it is less formal and no matter what age you are you will find yourself enjoying the experience.

Whatever you decide, do something spontaneous today, even if it is just giving someone a random hug or telling a joke if that is what is out of character for you. Surprise yourself today.

~

February 10th

What are you afraid of?

Lots of songs and poems have been written about our fears. They are mostly true. Whatever you are afraid of is rarely as bad as it seems to be. Imagining fear is often much worse than experiencing it. Remember in school the homework you hated? Which was worse thinking about it in the back of your head for hours or forty minutes just facing it and doing it? Often when we are afraid we think we are visualising how something will happen. In reality we are only guessing. Until the incident actually happens we have no way of knowing how it will turn out.

Every day if we can, or certainly once a week we need to do something that we are scared of. Sing out loud, voice an opinion, drive a car, wear the sexy top, face a foe or phone a friend. The fear may be tiny or huge to the outside world but to you it is everything. So do not let it control you. Overcome it. There is nothing to be frightened of. What's the worst that can happen? If you are still alive, then you will grow and learn from the experience. If it's a success you will be totally renewed.

Take a chance. Choose life. Don't waste it worrying over what may not happen (you have no control over this), what has happened (you have no control over this) or what might happen (I think you get the picture).

And if you feel rejected as if you have failed, after you make the effort, then own that feeling, deal with it and let it go, at the very least you will know that you tried.

~

February 11th

I think therefore I am

This wise old saying is as true today as ever. If you say "I feel awful, I am wrecked". Remove this phrase from your mind and ensure that it is gone forever. Why? Well your brain believes what you say and tries to make it real. Instead, tell yourself that "you feel wonderful and look lovely". Your mind shall not know the distinction.
Your mind is a very powerful tool and instinctively it believes whatever you think. So, see the world through a happy perspective and it will be all the more enjoyable. If you imagine how exhausted and unhappy you are it probably won't make any difference to how early you go to bed but it will affect how often you smile or laugh. Think you are happy and you will act happy. Think you are sad and you will act sad. If you act sad long enough you will start to feel sad. Conversely if you act happy, you will be happy even if only by accident. So, even if you are miserable or exhausted, concentrate on what you have and what you have achieved. Train your mind to think well of yourself and clap yourself on the back for everything you have accomplished. That is anything from a full night's sleep, to passing an exam at college or work, to toilet training a child. Every day we achieve so much and acknowledge our own worth to a much

lesser extent than we ought. So now, think and be the person you were born to be.
You know you deserve it.

~

February 12th

Express yourself

We all need a safe place where in to express ourselves. Some of us are lucky enough to live in a home where we can truly give vent to our feelings and emotions. Others are shy and do not always feel totally at ease proclaiming ourselves there. This is especially true if you live in a house share where you do not know the people that well and have just enough confidence for yourself to accept your ability, let alone any others. This is where art classes, drama groups, toastmasters and so on come in.
What better way to express what you love in a safe environment. In all of these sorts of groups everyone is there to develop their skill and their confidence at whatever level they may be today. There is no right or wrong answer to how you draw or paint. Alternatively maybe you always fancied speaking a foreign language or understanding the world under the bonnet of your car. Whatever it is express it in a safe place and have fun. It is a shame when hidden wishes to

enjoy a hobby (or even eventually pursue a career at it) remain out of sight just because we may have been knocked back in the past or fear that rejection generally. So take a leap of faith and ring up and inquire about that pottery evening, line dancing, Pilates, whatever it may be. At the very least it will broaden your horizons a little and at best it could prove a turning point in your existence.

~

February 13th

On enlarging what you want in another

People are what they are and we certainly cannot change them. What we can alter is who we are with. If you love tennis and then join a tennis club you have a great chance of meeting a tennis player. If you love books, go and join reading circles, visit libraries and book shops. The chances are that you will meet like-minded persons.
If you want to attract a generous man then become a generous woman. Whatever you wish to attract into your world you must first have grown in your own garden. People will see it and be drawn to it. As a result, you will end up with someone who is attracted to the qualities you cultivate, be they a new friend, a new boss or a new lover.
So, today, look at what you love. Go to work on it. Allow yourself the time and the opportunity to

enrich yourself and as if by magic watch what is drawn to you. It's amazing but true.

~

February 14th

On Valentine's Day

We may have all been there at one time or another sitting down maybe at a friend's house making the card (or watching them make one) or choosing endlessly in a card shop. Valentine's Day can, for some be great fun, full of attention, devotion and gifts.
Sadly, some of us nevertheless suffer the pain of unrequited love and if so it truly comes to a head today. All around us, all we think we can see are couples full of joy and completeness and us stark and alone. We try to understand the formula and allow ourselves to believe that a union with another will somehow complete us even though we know deep down that nothing is ever that simple and that we own our own happiness.
Valentine's Day can be tough. Tough if you're a couple and it's cold. Tough if you're alone and want to be a couple. Tough if you don't care and people keep telling you that you do. So today, do whatever you feel no matter how barmy. If you are deep in a loving relationship, then revel in the day. Alternatively if you are not, buy yourself

something pretty and enjoy it, be your own Valentine. At that point anything else will just be a bonus.

~

February 15th

This is your shot

For me I have just grasped at thirty eight years of age that I am about halfway through my life. I am starting to think about what I have done, what I have achieved. If I died today what would anyone remember me for? What would I like them to remember me for?

What about you? Today, have a little think about where you are in your existence. Are you following the path that you feel you were born to walk? Have you taken detours that have been good or that maybe are wasting your precious time? Right now I have about half my life left to live (if I am lucky). The first half was spent finding my feet. Feeling my way sometimes cautiously through life. I have made mistakes and taken a number of wrong turnings. Now, finally, at almost middle age, I can see the road ahead. I hope that I have the courage to walk ahead carrying in my little backpack all I have learned and unlearned along the way.

This is your shot. Don't waste your life living it for someone else. Live it for you. Start really living it today. Take chances and grab life pulling hard. Hold on tight and don't let go, you know when decisions feel right. Go for it and take your shot.

~

February 16th

You know who you are

You are not what you do. It is who you are that defines you, the invisible you. At times we feel that when what we do is not amazing then our lives are monotonous and that we should be doing something remarkable. Yet in our own small way we are keeping the world turning and doing great. We are who we are and we do not change depending on what we do. Therefore whoever you were at the start you are still that person. No matter what you do you cannot change that. And that is good.
Those that choose to judge you on occupation, appearance or circumstances are not true friends. True friends accept you as a person not a circumstance. Sometimes it is puzzling for even yourself not to judge you by what you do. Just remember, remember the little girl inside, the excited child who planned to be a solicitor or a teacher or whatever. Well she is still in there somewhere. You just have to find her.
Think back to when you were about ten. That's you

before the world got to you. That's how you are. She was lovely then as you are lovely now. The essence of you is timeless, the true you is eternal. Even after you part from your body, your soul/spirit will pass to a better place and continue on for ever. Your body is only a passing carrier. Your job or home or lifestyle is just now, just here. You, before you die, will live many lives and perform many roles. You will still be you just in altered situations. Think of how wonderful you are and leave behind those who are impressed only by what you do. Who you are is your contribution to this planet and that never changes. You are who you are.

~

February 17th

On the little things

It is the little things that can make or break any relationship. So the little things are very important. Relationships that have stood the test of time rarely fall apart over something big it is a rather gradual erosion of love due to small events left unnoticed that builds up.
An unusual characteristic that drew you to a loved one at the outset that you thought was quirky or cute may now be getting on your nerves more than ever. Maybe they never hang up their jacket and

leave it thrown somewhere or always leave a mess behind them in the kitchen. Over time this can grate on you and, though a small factor in a relationship, this can get right under your skin.

Therefore, you need to realise that every bed you make, every face you clean, means you are helping another and you must try not to get bogged down by those little things. Try and enjoy these rituals. When you get into your stride, then it remarkably becomes fun. Playing music/singing while you work can be a great help also.

Of course I am all for everyone in your life doing their bit and that encourages a strong, democratic home and work life. I am not suggesting that you encourage people not to pull their weight. We often feel upset as females, left with the little things to do. Doing little things continuously can get on your nerves and yet they are often dumped on us. Like changing towels, emptying the bin, wiping surfaces down, changing beds and much more. So know your importance and know their importance but try and keep it in perspective and not let the little things get to you too much.

~

February 18th

A brilliant idea

You waken up and have a brilliant idea. And do

not know what to do about it, where to go with it. It could be a brilliant invention, a critical business idea or even a great holiday. All through every day it rattles around in your head. You do not know what to do with it. Well, here is what to do.

Whenever you have a spare moment on a bus, or train, or in a supermarket or a bank queue, imagine your idea. Visualise it all the time. Then take yourself back gradually from the idea, step by step, until you are back where you started, with a great idea. You feel so much better and now you know how to implement it. If the route is a little fuzzy than enlist help from whoever would know, search the Internet, go to a library, ask around, whatever it takes.

If you believe it is still worth making into a reality then make up your perfect idea and play it out in your head whenever you can. Each time will be slightly different as it becomes finally tuned.

Maybe you could try something easy to start with and as you get braver something harder. It is a great adventure you must take, you owe it to yourself.

~

February 19th

If you love me let me go

This time I don't mean people. It is a spring clean

time of year. We all know about loving someone and letting them go and if it is right, then back they come (Or so they say!).

Well, it works with objects too! They call this "The law of the universe". Putting it plainly if you want nice dresses then find a lovely one you have and give it away. Now you won't get ten back just like it. However, you will get back many things, maybe some other piece of clothing that you really want. By then you may have forgotten how this all started and you will be thrilled to get the nice surprise of something coming your way unexpectedly.

The first few times I tried this I was a bit nervous. But once I got more confidence it worked out fine. I now have much too much make up, perfume and bathy stuff and I am thrilled.

The flip side of this is equally true. Belongings that I have held onto because I would not give them away or let someone else have them, well they just sit in my wardrobe staring at me as a reminder of how stingy I was that day. I can get no real pleasure from using them as they make me think of how mean I was. The other things that have come my way are a great sense of joy and fun and you know what? The things I gave away that I deliberated over for ages; well I cannot even remember what exactly they were now.

~

February 20th

Watch their eyes

Of everyone you come in contact with, watch their eyes. Do this for a day or two with all the people that you meet and soon you will know so much more about your family, friends and work colleagues. Eye contact means so much in an unspoken way. We do not truly trust someone who will not look us in the eye and we refer to them as shifty. Similarly a person who has an open face and looks us straight in the face inspires confidence in us even before they speak.
Everyone's eyes naturally land on what they love when they enter a room. Something generally catches their eye. Watch where their eyes travel and you will learn so much more about them. If you can, then offer them a little bit of what they love.

~

February 21st

Don't worry

Most of my fears are based on negative thinking: situations that I cannot change the outcome of anyway as they haven't happened yet and may never happen. Yet a part of me is almost imagining them. When I reach that point in my head then it is usually time for avoiding situations due to a fear of what might happen.

When I take the fear out to have a proper look at it I realise that it is empty and silly. However, inside me, it is a surreal power that can almost freeze me. Logical thought goes out the window and fear reigns. Thinking it out makes it worse because I am entertaining something non-existent. My solution is simple - I take the fear out of it and look at the predicament with a logical mind, asking for spiritual guidance. Then I realise (and not for the first time) that we all worry about situations but it is better not to, as we lose the chance to enjoy the now. And then I do my best to concentrate on that.

~

February 22nd

On early mornings

It can be tough to get up in the dark in winter. But, in reality there is nothing like the early morning. Coming down the stairs in the dark sometimes reminds me of Christmas morning. Seeing the sunrise as you organise your breakfast can be magical. For me I love hearing the birds that live on our roof waking and I try to remember to leave the remains of last night's dinner out for them on the bird table.

By getting up earlier than I used to I have noticed a few facts

1. The first thing you eat or drink in the morning always tastes yummy.

2. You have a clear head for planning your day.

3. There is something safe about early mornings that can hardly touch you.

I find with mornings when I am up late (that is after 7.30am) there is just no time. No time to think or plan or prepare or even relax into the day. When by the demands of a teething child or my own body clock I am up, then I use the time to set myself up for a nice day. Maybe I might read a thought for the day or do a little meditation, generally preparing to face the world.

I believe that a few positive thoughtful moments early on can benefit you right throughout the day, in making everything seem simpler and the day pass happier.

When the season changes and summer comes and it is bright I hope to take a little walk early. This will clear the cobwebs out for the day. We all know that there is nothing like a good night's sleep but also there is absolutely nothing as self-satisfying as wakening early, and facing the day on your own terms.

You have time to ponder, time to choose an outfit, not just throw one on. There is time to grab some spiritual food, time to eat a decent breakfast and time to plan something nice to look forward to for that evening, when your day's work is done.

~

February 23rd

On your weakness

We all have a weakness. It could be shoes, handbags, makeup or all three. For me it is the whole gel lotion thing and then the makeup, make up brushes and more hand and body lotions. It sounds so daft when I write it out but for me it is the most natural thing in the world.
In our wardrobe I have a huge gear bag. When you open it up the waft of exquisite bath products fill the room. I have oil burners, incense and candles in there too, also favourite cards, lovely hankies and oddments that I have picked up over the years.
I got the idea from a book I was reading about having plenty. So, when people asked what I wanted for a celebration I would say bath substances and I started building up a collection. It has been great fun finding out what fragrances I like and then what they remind me of. Some are the very essence of a fresh morning some are real winter or summer evening. The really precious ones I only use on special occasions.
I have a friend who has a weakness for handbags. She has truckloads of them hidden under her bed. I have never seen her with the same handbag. They

are all lovely and very fashionable. She has a sister who is obsessed with makeup and skin care. And I do mean obsessed! The handbag one finds the makeup chats boring and snorts when it begins, handbag lady loves books and her bedroom is lined with them.

I adore spending time with both of them because they have such contrasting personalities and are so engaging.

I love analysing make up and skin care with them. I also love books and so we all have a great deal to chat about.

I have another girlfriend who just loves to buy underwear. She cannot even step out into an underwear section without coming away with a purchase. However she is not big on make-up.

I suppose what I am really saying is that I love being a girl and I hope you do too. What is your weakness? It may not even have been mentioned here but the great thing about being a girl is that there is always someone out there with whom to share your weakness.

~

February 24th

Obvious

Sometimes how we feel and how we fix it is just so obvious, that we miss it. We talk about having common sense and yet often the first answer is the right one and we just keep searching and digging, looking for a hidden meaning.

If I feel like I need a friend then I need a friend. If I feel like I am overtired then I need more sleep. This sounds obvious but so often we have a feeling and are upset and we go looking for a solution to what is really a much uncomplicated problem.

Rather than analysing the whys and wherefores of the dilemma we should start with something simple and see how we get on. If we are always unhappy at this time of year then we can pre-empt that by planning. Maybe a few nice treats for ourselves or a weekend away or getting into the sales: whatever will provide us with the life we need. Solutions are usually quite obvious if only we look at them and stop searching deeply for a hidden meaning which may not even be there.

~

February 25th

Criticism

Fault finding is a tricky situation. Some people have knowledge in an area and can give an accurate general criticism. This may be of a subject or event yet even then it is just their perception and so it is not infallible.

Other people are always available to provide

criticism. It is often given without full knowledge or by request from the receiver. When you receive criticism like this we need to be careful. Look at the motivation of the person behind the comment. Too often we are put off by a casual criticism that they may not even remember saying a day later. We, however, can be affected and may allow this to stop us from living positively.

With that in mind, criticism from a trusted party is worth its weight in gold and can save us a lot of time and waste. It can also help us with direction and honing our craft whatever that may be. So, beware the random critic and their motivation yet listen to what the professional has to say and take just what you need away with you.

~

February 26th

You have got loads

Now even though you have maybe given away some possessions you have loads of stuff. No matter how you sometimes feel that you don't have enough. Well, let me tell you, you have loads. Maybe loads of what you don't want but you have loads. Think about the basic things you think you need and look at what you have. If you have more than one of anything you are doing well. When we feel we haven't enough we are comparing ourselves with others but we can never fully see what they have or don't have. Trust me you have loads.

Now, if you believe me and think it too, you will not thank me! Soon your place will be cluttered up with more and more as what you think about expands. So if you hated that jumper and thought about it a lot you probably have a few similar ones. Well think about lovely sandals or fabulous scented perfumes and watch them flock to you. I always think of how I have loads of lovely soaps and grooming products and I have. It really works, just be careful what you wish for.

~

February 27th

On music

I have a friend who has music for every occasion. When she is getting ready to go out with her friends she plays loud dance music. When she is preparing a beautiful meal she has been heard playing the Three Tenors. When she is going to sleep she plays soft restful music.

Music in your life provides depth and colour to every situation. Soft music, in the background when you have friends over, creates a lovely mood. Lively music makes you want to get up and dance.

Children all over the world love music. That speaks

volumes. Music is another of life's miracles. There are only so many notes yet there is always new music. Angels are generally associated with music and music's divine power should never be underestimated.

In most religions music plays an important role. It brings us all together in the moment and lifts our spirits and rests our souls.

We all need music. Even if we think we can't sing or hate what we hear we must search until we find our sound. When we do we will be soothed and calm, still as a feather on a pond. Just let the music begin.

~

February 28th

On miracles

Many times in my life I have found myself saying that something is a miracle and being amazed when it all works out. Oh me of little faith in life. Miracles are sometimes remarkable huge worldwide events bringing sceptics and religious together and drawing world-wide attention. In my experience, while those miracles are wonderful, miracles mostly go almost unnoticed. For example: I have gotten so used to asking for a parking space and getting it, I would hardly count that as a miracle anymore when believe me it often is.

A seed that sits in a pot and grows into a beautiful scented flower is certainly a miracle and is difficult to explain even if you are a botanist. A child born with perfect hands, feet and all moving parts working correctly is a miracle that happens every day around the world. Yet, so often we are searching for something unusual, something dramatic and we miss the miracles taking place in the world around us.

Someone addicted to a substance who through self-help groups, counselling and support manages to go clean, well that is a miracle all on its own.

So today, look around you at what surprises you. For every bad and sad situation you see there are many more wonderful, miraculous circumstances going on right in front of your eyes. You just need to see them for what they are- Miracles.

~

MARCH

March 1st

On laughter

People talk about laughter lines. Well, a face tells a story all its own and there is nothing worse than a face with a frown. We often nearly laugh despite ourselves. It is almost like we think maybe it is better to be serious. When in fact, humour draws people together and unites the most unlikely liaisons. Have you ever seen two people talking earnestly and in observing them you think that they are most likely arguing and the next moment they both roar laughing. Or someone who tells you a joke and starts to laugh and you find yourself caught up in their infectious laughing even though you have hardly got the joke at all.
Laughing is so contagious. It is hard to be sad when you are laughing. Now and then circumstances can seem so bad that you will either laugh or cry. Unless you literally truly feel you have no alternative then I would suggest that you laugh. It lightens the load and is what we were born to do. The best nights out or in, that you have ever had, I guarantee you, included a great laugh. Then there are the sombre times like wakes. Most Irish people flock to these as the craic is great, laughing and remembering the dead and so honouring their memory. Someone always says he/she would want us to be happy he/she would want us to laugh.

So today, pretend to laugh and so you will. Look up a few corny jokes and share them. See how your face relaxes and your jaw drops. You probably now feel so much better.

~

March 2nd

Savour the day

Even if it is a seemingly really boring day that you are facing, try and see the beauty in it.
If it is a meeting you had to attend for the umpteenth time or a match you have to watch in the freezing cold, whatever it is suppose in your head that it is either the first or the last time that you will do it. That helps you to be in the now. Otherwise we can all tend to veer off thinking about what to cook for dinner, or who we need to email and so on.
But when you see something for the first time you really look closer instead of taking it for granted. If I saw my car for the first time: the sun roof, the headrests, the hub caps, objects that I don't even see day to day when I approach and sit in the vehicle, they would be really obvious. When people I know are speaking to me I am rarely savouring their words I am generally thinking about my comment and what will happen next. Today I am going to try and savour each precious moment as

best as I can, without even accidentally wishing it away. Most likely we will get many more days but we never know. So we must savour each one for it is precious.

~

March 3rd

Moods

You know, when you are sure that a day is going to be good or bad, you are rarely disappointed. If you approach a situation in good form oozing a good mood your positive outlook will relax the most stressed mind.
If you approach the same occasion in a bad mood the bad karma can fill the room in seconds even before you have uttered a single word, even if you don't mean it to.
A happy, open outlook can trickle through everything and touch everyone even if only in a small way.
When you are in a bad mood you think it is just you that is down. It can, however upset all those around you-Even if you don't mean it to.
So today be like I will and practice being in good form despite everything that has happened is happening or may happen and see how much easier life is as a result.

~

March 4th

What's your favourite colour?

My favourite colour rotates from dark red to blue and back again with an occasional twist of pale pink. I wonder what that says about me.
If you don't know your favourite colour find out what it is. Go to a pretty boutique and try on lots of tops and see which one you like. See what colour really brightens up your face. Some colours drain you, some cheer you up some comfort you. Some colours make you feel more confident than others.
So what is your preferred colour at the moment? It changes all the time depending on what is going on in your life or what mood you are in. Reds are passionate colours, blues are serene and cool, purples are creative and intriguing, pinks well they are just great fun.
So, have a little look around and see what colour catches your eye today. Have fun with it. When you find a new tint try different shades in makeup, bags, shoes and clothes.
Notice how much better you look in a colour that suits you: One that you feel happy in.
If you work in an office of black suits, buy a red one or yellow or whatever colour you like or if you are not brave enough to go all the way maybe a bright scarf or shirt. You will be remembered for being you. So embrace what you love, hunt out your

shade, the one that best suits you and wear it with pride, after all it is your favourite colour.

~

March 5th

That special something

When you discover/have chosen your special style, people will notice it not just because things may look changed on you or your home, but because of that certain "Je ne sais quoi", that special something. It is impossible to put your finger on it or exactly explain it but it is your mark. And when we are being genuine, even just with ourselves, it makes us or our home seem more appealing. People are drawn to the authentic and may tell you there is something different about you. Did you get your hair done differently? Was that couch always there? What it really is is you being you and that's irresistible to all the right people. So, let it be and let your taste shine through, your home will look lovely and you will never be lonely.

~

March 6th

Surround yourself with light

We, animals, plants, everything, we all need light to survive. We are no exception. We need to be surrounded by people of light. If you surround yourself with negative thinkers, you begin to think a little like them and lose a little of your joy. Surround yourself with light hearted people who don't take themselves too seriously. Be encouraged by their positive outlook. As you talk to them you will realise they too have enjoyed lives ups and downs, tragedies and joys. The distinction between them and others is they look to the light and take a positive from a negative. Be like them and use their guiding light to shine you on your journey. Keep the negative thinkers who put ideas and people down, to a minimum. Do not let that cloud your view of life. Now I am not saying you have to be happy all the time, far from it. I am just suggesting that you fill your surroundings with joy not misery. It helps to lighten the load if your surround yourself with light.

~

March 7th

Expectation

I was re-reading an old diary that I found today and I was shocked at how low my expectations were. The strange thing is I ought to have been thrilled because I had easily surpassed the expectations of those five years ago. However the main problem with expectations is that we aim too low and succeed so easily. I compared my expectations of today to the old ones of five years ago and realised great challenges are ahead at least in order to reach today's goals. They are called expectations because I expect them. From here on in there can be few surprises, I expect the unexpected. I am aiming high so if at first I don't succeed, I miss my step, I won't fall far. Five years ago I aimed low and succeeded, then for five years I wondered why I was not progressing. You yourself must have expectations of you. It is no good thinking what others expect of you, it is your life so expect it to be brilliant. Expect it to be what you believe it should be and whatever you deserve. Then set about making it happen.

~

March 8th

Nature

There is something oddly relaxing about nature. So much so that, shops sell sounds of the ocean to relax tired babies and adults download sounds of rivers and rain.
In life all we sometimes need to do is to open a window. Five minutes spent listening quietly to nature is just so relaxing. If you live in the country you are then bound to at least hear a bird singing or the wind rustling through the leaves of a tree. In

the city you may need to search for a park or a small green area. Even in the busiest places they generally exist. Mind you at lunchtime they are always full. They are full because we all yearn for that connection with nature during our day. If you are lucky enough to have a balcony or private garden, try and put a few pots of flowers out and promise yourself at least five minutes during the day in it. Notice the colour, the growth, the atmosphere. Make it your sanctuary; it brings peace to a restless soul. If all you have is a window buy a window box, fill it with fragrant flowers and close your eyes and you could be anywhere you wish. Take time to appreciate nature, for it is the earth we come from and to the earth our bodies return.

$\sim$

March 9th

Simple fun

We all know how rich people go on about not needing money to have simple fun. We also know that money takes the sting out of things. Even though parks, beaches, hill walks are all free we still look at the floor and try to change the subject when people lecture us on this. Well I have news. There is a simpler funnier fun to be had and it doesn't have to be found outdoors or in exercise.
Now I know that exercise has an important place in

healthy living and clearing your mind and so on. Notwithstanding that sometimes you just might not want to exercise or it is raining or snowing, so what can you do?

Well, my first port of call is the makeup counter. They all do free makeovers, some on the spot and some by appointment. You get all made up for nothing and also get advice on skincare and colours that suit and maybe even complimentary samples. It is great fun and can be very interesting. I usually book ahead, create an atmosphere. The main thing is I walk away feeling great, looking much better than on arrival.

Another fab treat is doing a night-time thing during the day. Cinema by day can feel so exhilarating. Try sitting mid-week in a cinema watching a thriller, munching popcorn while the world's wheels continue to turn without you. Try it, it is fantastic. Or try treating yourself to fresh flowers from the street sellers. Wandering around shops and trying on clothes and imagining where you would go in them can be fun too. It is even greater fun if you have company. It is a good chance to see what suits you and what taste you have.

And finally, if you have children or young relations I would strongly advise child's play. No one midway through doing a blue foot print on a white sheet of paper is ever stressed. Hand and feet painting is tremendous as a relaxation tool. You become totally immersed in it and the children are thrilled to see you so messy. So get thinking, make a list. What do you do for simple fun or what would you like to do?

~

March 10th

On international women's day

Today was International Women's day however on this day I did not feel like an international woman. I felt the same as ever. I went to work, I cleaned, I cooked, I read, I wrote. I got to be all the things a woman can be except I felt ordinary and I feel this day is for someone special out there; someone who is having a big adventure far away from me. All that is wrong and I know it.

International Woman's day is for all of us, it is just that we must find the time to get out there and grab it. It is sadly not coming looking for us. No one will tell us how great we are except another who has walked our walk. Every one of us has the right to stand on a podium at a world women's conference and tell our story. We are all brave and courageous and are very special. But we need to know this and remind each other. We must support each other and then there is some hope of the rest of the world finding out how good we are.

Today, celebrate who you are, a woman. You may not feel amazing right now but you are. You have worked hard to reach the place you are in and you know you have a long way to go. Take your lunch-break buy a fancy coffee or a sticky bun or a pretty flower whatever you like. Congratulate yourself. Remember it wasn't easy for our Grandmothers and our Mums before us but this generation are as busy so whatever you have achieved feel proud and celebrate it. This is your day. Sit back and reflect what it means to you and vow that next year you will be ready. Set some time aside for you as this is your day too.

~

March 11th

Clean the problem out!

Clean the problem out! We are back at our homes again. The state of your home is meant to represent your state of mind. Big messy home means big messy head. Now my home is far from show house conditions. Sometimes it runs away on me.-clothes piling up, dishes queuing up. Then I start to feel like I am not coping well and so the mess escalates. It is like a self-fulfilling prophecy. The cure is just one big problem. You know when something really big in your life is happening and you don't know what to do about it.

Well for all of these encumbrances I recommend "housework". They can be no therapy like throwing out old rubbish, clearing cluttered spaces or really cleaning a bathroom. When we become truly immersed in cleaning the mind stops concentrating on the problem, this gives your subconscious a chance to come up with an alternative solution.

As your home starts to look more normal you start to pick up more. Your home feels more like the sanctuary it should be and less like the mess that it was. It is lovely after a stressful day to relax in a clean tidy home. Then, you can, surprisingly, enjoy your home-which can otherwise be hard to do when everywhere you look you see something you feel that you should do. As you see each room take shape you will be surprised at what you don't want or don't need any more and shocked at how good it feels. Every tidy room brings you one step closer to a tidy mind.

Even if your problem is not solved you will have had time to digest it. It is very difficult to think clearly sitting in a hazy mess. Your state of mind is in your hands- you alone decide how you feel -so feel good, have your home look good, it is much less fun to be miserable.

~

March 12th

You can change your world

We all live in this world but it is altered for all of us. Obviously, if you live in a first world country or in a third world country then your life condition will be different. Similarly if you live in wet Dublin or hot Las Vegas you are going to be affected by the climatic variance. However, even if you live only two doors away from somebody on the same road or in an apartment block your lives can be drastically different. Sometimes, when I am out walking I peep into open doorways or windows as I pass by other people's homes. Some homes contain old world, dark furniture, lots of patterned ornaments. Some are modern, sleek designs that are clean cut. Some are classically styled and some are traditional. On the outside most are identical. There is more than one way to live. Understand what suits you. Obviously there is a basic framework of order, however apart from that the world is your oyster. So even if you do not want to move home you can create a habitat that really reflects you. Who we are speaks volumes in our choice of covers, paint work, pictures, tea sets, duvet covers, cushion covers and so on. These items need not be financially expensive yet they can drastically change the perception of a home. Let your home reflect you and whoever lives there.

Then you will feel truly at home whether it be in a house, an apartment or a bed-sit.

~

March 13th

It is a bit like shopping

Did you ever fill out a survey in a supermarket asking why you shopped there? Quality, value, availability and so on were the variables offered to you. Well that's life. Except we want it all and we want it now. Well, you have got to decide which item on the menu you want to achieve firstly and set about obtaining it. If you want value more than anything else you must look at how you appraise things. Most importantly how do you value yourself? Are you good enough to you? Do you really appreciate those around you every day and do you value the contributions they make to your varied life. Then look at how you spend your time. Time is so precious it must be valued for there is never enough. So make sure you value yourself. Remind yourself what a wonderful package and gift you are. Tell yourself positive things about yourself regularly. Only when you truly value yourself can you begin to value everybody else. For then you know you are worthy.

~

March 14th

What do you like?

Think of something swimming or tennis, for instance, or make up or news or movies or theatre, whatever really interests you. If you like it you might even be good at it. If you like it you probably know a fair bit about it. Well did you know, it is easier to make money from something you love? Say you love Tennis. Well, if you choose not to play in competitions or coach then you could write a sports column or commentate at matches or present a television programme on Tennis or many other careers: these are just a few ideas. So think today what do I love about life? Whatever jumps into your head think of all the careers associated with it and see what appeals to you. The chances are that you will choose one that you know you will be good at. Now you just have to figure out how to get from here to there. That is unless you are a rare commodity or person and already love to bits what you are doing. If that's not the case then you must first look at what you love and then look at how to get paid for doing it! All you need is a little imagination and a great deal of determination.

~

March 15th

Tidy house, tidy mind

Anyone who knows me will laugh at this one as I have a young family and tidiness is the least of my worries. Even so, of an evening I can be found putting things away, cleaning down surfaces and giving order to my world. I find that when my environment is generally tidy I can think more clearly and see things in my mind better. Otherwise, there I am thinking about say planning a week-end away when the ironing jumps into my head. I find, though that when the house is vaguely under control it frees up my mind for more interesting excursions of imagination. Today, I am being interviewed by a minor celebrity (well in my mind!), it goes very well and I can really relate to her! Far more than I can to the pile up after dinner in our kitchen! A home has a life and an energy all its own, it should be cared for as it is a very significant part of your world. It is one you inhabit every day so do not see it as a waste of time. Rather see it as making your world more welcoming, nicer, and more enjoyable so that then when you open the door to come in it greets you just as you like it: ready for you to jump in and enjoy.

~

March 16th

March

I sometimes wonder if it is called that because in Ireland it is the month when most of us hit the ground running so to speak. In June in Dublin there is a women's mini marathon 10k in length and most evenings from now on the paths are filled with women walking two by two. All shapes all sizes take to the streets walking briskly. Some are chatting incessantly others wearing MP3 players, others totally silent. All are engaging in a great pursuit in one way or another. Walking is the best exercise for all ages. It requires only open space and decent footwear. It gets us out of the home and clears our minds. While we concentrate on the walking at a good pace and doing our thirty minutes or whatever our nightly quota is, our minds are renewed enough by the change in scenery as we walk thus allowing our sub conscious minds to process our thoughts and difficulties. After every walk we come back rejuvenated, refreshed and we feel really good about ourselves. If we do the marathon we are also helping a charity so it is doubly good. Not to mention all of the fun that comes from being a part of something bigger than ourselves. Everyone who finishes the marathon receives a medal no matter how long they take to complete. So there are no losers. So think about it. If not for the fitness, then to clear your head, or to have a valid excuse to hook up with a friend! You could contact a charity you admire and walk for them from your area. You may even end up making new local friends from the experience. Whatever way you work it this is the season to March.

~

March 17th

St. Patrick's Day

This is the day when tourists sit in ridiculous traffic jams in small towns and wonder what the hell is going on. This is our day. It is our national day of celebration. This is a day when we are truly proud of our being Irish and it is celebrated all over the world and not just here on the Island of Ireland. Parades are held throughout the country and the biggest parade is held in a different continent altogether. This reminds me that so many of us are scattered all over the universe. Some of my family are just a couple of thousand miles away others are more than six thousand. Even though we are far apart we are united in celebration. In another way we are all connected and feel closer than ever. Our small town holds a parade all its own. If it is sunny we will stand at the roadside and wave it by, if it rains as it often does we will huddle under a shop entrance, bush or car and watch from afar. Whatever we do we know it is a special day, and as we watch the dancers, acrobats and musicians from nations far and wide walk with us in our parades we know it is not just us who are celebrating. We are united with countries where fathers bordered boats and planes to find work and where sons travelled, fell in love and where family ties stretch far across seas and land. All of them, today, are stopping for, maybe, even just a few instants and remembering that they are Irish. Céad míle fáilte.

~

March 18th

Availability

We are getting to know who we are and now we are thinking more clearly what we want from life. Things are often not available when we want them. What to do about that? Whatever you want available to you and cannot have do not despair of getting it. See it as achieved already in your mind. The mind is a powerful tool where we can imagine to our hearts content unknown to those around us and it is a great way to help us make things happen. In your daily life act as if you are the sort of person you would be if you had whatever you are looking for. Gradually the shift will occur as your mind pushes to make it real and through generosity and determination it will begin to be drawn to you. Watch for it and welcome it when it comes. For certain, it is just a matter of when you will obtain it.

~

March 19th

Keeping your word

Never underestimate the power of keeping your word. If you have family or work colleagues or anyone you interact with habitually and you are a woman of your word they will learn to respect what you say and believe in you.
Your partner or friend will know that you mean what you say and that he can count on you in any situation.
Alternatively, if you do not always stand by your word and just agree to keep everyone happy for that moment then no one knows where they stand with you. Children are confused and insecure not really knowing their boundaries and people in general will be slower to trust in you. Society at large has trust at the core, so often we hand over ourselves and our families to people based on what they promise. It can be something as simple as a hair salon and your hair or something as serious a child minder and your precious child.
It can be tricky at first to keep our word if it is not

convenient however it is really just another habit. If you ask someone for a favour and they agree and you trust them to deliver it then it is a great weight off your mind. If you can't trust them then you will be wondering if they will let you down or should you check or chase them just in case. That does not feel right now does it?

So, be a woman of this world and keep your word, after all your word is your bond.

~

March 20th

How do you look?

I have a crooked face. When I wear glasses (one ear is lower than the other) they have to be adjusted to look straight on my face. One side of my face (if you looked at a photo) is slightly different than the other though generally it is the same. Following on, my chest is two different sizes and so are my feet.

Now, I could get upset over these flaws in my appearance (especially the ear bit) (dangly earrings always look a little funny!) but I prefer the philosophy that someone someday somewhere will be looking for someone just like me and there I'll be.

If we all changed ourselves to match a coded look, then no one would look real and no one would be wanted for television, magazines or any media.

I hope you can relate to me. My teeth slightly protrude, I have large wide unladylike feet, I am not tall. I am pale. I have freckles. I am going grey. (I am laughing now- this reads really badly). But here is the thing-I love me. I love the bones of me. I am witty, cynical, passionate, a little judgmental, interesting and excited by life. You can be too. Just accept yourself as in my case lopsided and all.

~

March 21st

Foodstuffs

Take a stroll through your nearest town someday soon and you will marvel at all the different eateries. In Ireland now there are many traditions of cooking represented in our cafes and restaurants. There are even restaurants dedicated to gluten free, dairy free, and obviously meat free.

Just as every hand print in the world is unique so we all have slightly and not so slightly contrary tastes or requirements in food. Naturally there are overlaps and thank goodness for that because then we can all break bread together. There is nothing comparable to sitting down to a meal with friends or family. Once we begin to enjoy our meal the conversation becomes more relaxed and we can really interact with each other.

We all need to eat at one time or another. We have

been blessed with vibrant taste buds. Savouring new tastes slowly in your mouths is a true treat. In general we do not taste even half of the food we eat. It is taken on autopilot.

This week think about different foods you have never tried. Pick out a few to try with the ones you like, savour the taste, notice the colour and texture and really start to enjoy the food. Make food fun, not just a chore. It is an adventure that's generally safe to take and genuinely rewarding.

~

March 22nd

On advice

Some people go around asking a lot of people's advice about the same problem until they get the answer they want and then they take that advice.

Some people ask just one person and then take their advice.

Some people trust half the people and ask their advice and digest it with their own for their solution.

Advice is a strange thing. It is difficult for anyone to be impartial as their own experience and thoughts cloud their judgement. Advice, however, can be useful so as to provide a contrary perspective to stew on with a sticky problem.

For me, for advice, I usually need to consult one

trusted friend. Then I do the right thing and go within. I hand it over mentally and try and trust that over the next few days an answer will come to me. There can be many answers to any one situation and I generally pray for guidance that I am led to the best one for me.

So, be careful with receiving and giving advice-for we rarely know best for another though we always think we do.

~

March 23rd

On age

I looked in the mirror this evening and for the first time I realised that I was certainly getting older. I remember about two weeks after my thirtieth birthday when I saw the first line appear at my left eye. I was horrified! This seems very funny now.

Back to today, I remember my friend told me that her mum was talking to her about how she remembers the time when people stopped looking at her in the street and workmen stopped whistling at her. I suppose we all think people will always notice us and those who flirt will continue to flirt with us throughout the retail outlets of the world. In fact the day comes to us all as women when it is time to start to grow up gracefully.

I know that I may live another forty years however

for me already the Gardaí look about sixteen, Top of the pops is mostly a mystery and chat rooms a different species.

So I looked in the mirror and realised that my face is changing. I am starting to look less like I did as a child and young woman and more like me. If I study my face I can see it is made up of all my experiences in whatever way I have processed them. I notice the positive hope in my eyes, the deep smile and my earnest wishes. I can gradually see that over time I am emerging to look on the outside like I am feeling on the inside.

Now I must prepare to let go the ego, let go the feeling of loss and embrace me and all I have to offer as I finally enter proper maturity it seems for the first time.

So whether you are twenty, thirty or sixty take a peek at your face. Spot the pretty bits. Rejoice in them. Indulge the process and welcome your true self home.

~

March 24th

Courage

Courage takes many forms. The word seems gigantic. We imagine lions, tigers, wars and other big events. Courage can be as simple as looking in the mirror and being brave enough to face who you really are and loving it. Really seeing ourselves not how others do but in reality. Courage can be standing up to someone who is acting badly towards you and believing you are worth it. Courage can mean being scared before, during and after the event but doing it anyway. Courage can mean many things but once we begin to let it into our lives we can start to see, with courage comes a responsibility for our actions and a thrilling independence. We are taking the control of our lives, we are accepting the consequences. We are being brave and we are being courageous.

~

March 25th

On beauty and age

I got a call from a friend the other day that surprised me. She was wondering why an expensive translucent moisturiser looked wrong on her skin. I found myself trying to explain about pigments in skin, people being seasons, how your natural hair colour is made to enhance your skin tones. My friend is really pretty and has all the products at her fingertips. She was having what another friend calls a lower self-day. She thought she could feel and see her age creeping up on her. We see the lines on our faces, the world sees the wisdom. We see the blemishes and shadings; the world sees our experiences and experience. We see that we have had children they see our feline curves. We see that we are top heavy they see an ample bosom. It is all in how you view it. As we grow older there is nothing more beautiful than seeing the real person emerge. If you look into the face of someone who has lived a good natural life, it is all in their face. When they have been badly hurt it is there too. Stare long enough and you know their whole story. Youth has its own beauty. Even so the beauty of a real self-assured mature woman is hard to compete with. So, though we all doubt ,we all have bits we do not like, we ought to remember we all have loved or have been loved, we have all lived. We have all experienced life and it is all there in our poor pale faces gorgeous and sparkling for the entire world to see.

~

March 26th

Feathers

It is said that if there are birds in your garden they are messengers from heaven. So if you find a white feather in your garden or on your car door or one land at your feet, there is an angel nearby thinking of you. If you consider it white feathers turn up in the oddest places and usually with not a trace of a bird. One day I found one on the seat of the car! I have met many people who believe in angels and some with sincere devotion. Others do not believe but it is rare to meet one person who does not want to. The whole concept of a winged one minding us and watching over us is very reassuring and beautiful. It brings with it a great sense of belonging and being wanted. So whether you are so connected that your angel has a name or so sceptical that you think it's daft, let the feathers fall where they may and let the birds be. Who knows what is going on and either way a little feather will do you no harm.

~

March 27th

On mother's day

Around now, the end of March two things will happen. Firstly, we welcome spring and pop our clocks on one hour. Our mornings will be brighter, our evenings longer and our mind is set for summer. Equally important is Mother's Day. You know what they say, the older you get the more your mother knows. When you were ten she knew everything. Then she forgot and for a decade knew nothing. Then she learnt a little. By thirty five she was really getting the hang of life. But then by forty when you finally knew she had the answers she was nearly gone. So before it is too late for you here are a few items that I have found out. Being a mum requires patience, monotony, patience and truck loads of understanding. Mums are rarely appreciated at the time. It is usually after the fact. Mums can spot a hungry face in the crowd, a sad face at a party, a cold hand on a hot day. I am not saying that they are perfect. They can be cranky, narky, tired, frustrated and often a little bitter. But it is the hand they are dealt that decides that. Treat your mum like a queen, bow to her wisdom and you will become wise. Treat a mum to her tea and she will always be grateful to you. Treat her to lunch and she will surely entertain you. Treat her to a night off and she will always thank you. Treat a mum to clothes and she will shop for you. Treat a mum well she is always there for you. Mums are the anchor even if there is only the two of you. They can make a family, create an atmosphere and blow a fuse in just the time it takes for you to get your coat off. So, stand for mums today, without them we would never exist. And if they are grumpy, make them laugh, and if they are sad, cuddle them. And if they are lonely, visit them. And if they have found happiness, be glad for them. Theirs is a full-time life time job, with lots of overtime, at no extra pay, and so much love you can only dream about.

~

March 28th

Dreams and ambitions

If you are a person who has dreams it can be very hard for everyone else around you. Whatever your concept you see it really clearly and they of course can barely see it. They are living in this reality and it is often tricky for them to jump to your new one. Be patient. If your idea has urgency, determination and a firm date you could be tricky to be around. The situation can become very intense for everyone else. Be patient with others. When times are good share your thoughts and dreams. Make them a part of the dream if you can. If you have older children include them and help them feel they are a part of it. Once they understand they will all clear a space in their lives for what you want. They all want you to be happy. It helps when they can understand what it is you want. Give them that responsibility. It is also true that this will encourage you to persevere and then if you give up, they will all know. So when you are ready tell those you trust and love the positive people in your life and watch them clear your path for you to achieve your dreams.

~

March 29th

On friends

Whatever age you are you need a friend. If you don't have any think of what you enjoy, go there and set about getting yourself someone to share it with. There is nothing like an old school friend. Maybe you have one friend that you have lost touch with and whose company you really enjoyed. Even if she lives far away, drop a note or call or email. Make a connection. She will probably be thrilled that you made the effort. Maybe you will just be phone friends for a while but that's okay too. It is lovely to know that there is someone pleased to get your call. Even if you have little in common you can both enjoy the diversity. As we get older we find it harder to bond in friendship. So much has gone before. But that's okay too. Some people have friends from work, friends from school or college friends, from a night class or a baby group. All have a part to play. They may not know where you came from but they know you today and we all need someone with whom to share our lives. Even if we are madly in love with a partner we still need space and within that space we need friends. If you have old ones that you have held on to you should be very thankful. Don't ever take them for granted. If they are new be appreciative and enjoy the place you share with them. And if you have yet to make any then be brave, step out. Join classes and groups engaging in hobbies that you enjoy and this will naturally draw you to like-minded people.

~

March 30th

Staying centred

Irrespective of what concerns and circumstances you are dealing with today, staying focused is the key to helping you enjoy it more. When we are focused we have compatibility and symmetry in our lives. We can remain calm in a crisis and generally we can make wise and appropriate decisions. This stops us also from getting annoyed over stupid little things. So, in turn, our home and personal lives run much more smoothly. So, how do we know if we are not centred? Well, if we feel quite stressed much of the time the chances are that we are putting our thoughts in the past or the future too often. When someone asks for our help we feel stressed as we are pondering what has to be done. If we were just focusing on the job in hand instead then we would be calmer, happier and more pleasant to be around. Those close to us would be delighted and helping someone out might not seem like such a big deal after all.

~

March 31st

Self esteem

As Irish people I believe we put each other down, frequently in front and behind our backs. Sometimes we do this in humour, sometimes to begrudge, often as an automatic reaction. This for a woman busy in her life does little to help her self-esteem. Her self- esteem is hidden inside and no one can see it. If self- confidence is lacking it can be bluffed fairly well and we can make it through most situations. However, if we don't get a grip on our self- esteem and look after it, it can be chipped away and cause blockages when we try and move forward in our lives.

Next time you get a spare few minutes look in the mirror. Recognise how well you look and tell yourself this. Smile at yourself and enjoy yourself. You will gradually feel the self- esteem grow as you continue positive communication with yourself. When you have given yourself enough confidence the knocks will bounce off and you will succeed more often than not.

We need to remind ourselves that we are strong independent people and successful too even if we have only just gotten out of bed. To succeed in calming the storms in our lives and our hearts we must first love the ship that is making our voyage. Know how brave and special you are. Love the person you are. Feck those who begrudge they will always be there. Make sure you give them a success to moan about. Start today.

~

As we travel into the final month of this season below is a reminder of some of the simple ideas we have looked at over February and March. Maybe we taken up some and left others, or not started at all, it is never too late….

- Plant seeds
- Make a treasure box
- Release our dreams
- Be spontaneous
- Express ourselves
- Be our own best friend
- Watch the little things
- Discover what we love-Clothes, colours, fabrics and styles
- Get enough light
- Accept ourselves (easier said than done)

APRIL

April 1st

April fool's Day

When we were children we got great fun out of this day and would often play all sorts of tricks on each other and if we were brave enough even on a few grown- ups. The jokes were traditionally played before Noon so if we had managed to escape till then we were unlikely to be tricked in person. This day is a reminder of how in some ways we are all alike and enjoy a bit of fun all over the world. Most national media get in on the idea and the great fun can be trying to guess what is real and what is not on the television or in the newspaper. The truth being often more confusing than fantasy makes this not as simple as it sounds. Years ago this day was on a small scale locally and in newspapers but with the World Wide Web it can take on huge proportions. So today, have a light heart and enter into the spirit of the moment. It takes a bit of character to allow a joke to be played on us and a bit of imagination to come up with an original new gag. Think of something funny and have a go, relive your youth and feel what it is like to laugh properly again.

~

April 2nd

What do you weigh?

You weigh nothing. Remember that your body weighs the same whether you are alive or dead, hence you, the real you, is weightless and that is all that counts. There is no measure of you, only within you. Therefore make sure you measure well and realise just how magical you actually are. You are eternal; you are not a part of your weighted body which heads off into the sunset when you die. So be good to you and do not worry too much about your body weight. Your body is NOT you. You are your personality, your soul, your spirit, and no-one can put a measure or a weight on that. Your body is merely a chamber to house you on this earth. Mind it and it will last longer. But don't feel pressurized into fussing over your body as its not who you are. You are much more. Almost everyone in the public eye is now dipping into injections and surgery to prolong the appearance of slim youth. Yet this does not change the amount of time they spend here on earth. It also does not change their eternal selves, which are timeless, the person within. I remember when I was younger and looking in the mirror to see the first line appear around my eye. I was gutted and felt the onset of age. Now I would be thrilled with that one line. My physical self is never either just how I would like it, but it does not matter. My face at close quarter's looks much better than it did back then without the aid of any implants or nips and tucks. My secret new phrase: happier inside always looks better outside and the realisation that the real things that matter are weightless.

~

April 3rd

The promise of summer

I hope by now you have planted some seeds and that they are starting to pop up to see you. If not it's still not too late if you plant this week. You can still have summer blooms. This is a lovely time of year. The evenings are brighter and longer and the promise of summer beckons. It is like two extra hours have been added into the day. Make the most of it. Get out for an evening stroll or eat your evening meal "Al fresco" or better still sit outside and watch the sun setting. There is something about sunrise and sunset that helps you see the cycle of life. It is very beautiful and very soothing. If you are lucky enough to have a little garden and it is overgrown, rejoice in the wild flowers, butterflies and ladybirds that greet you. If it's well maintained the calm is there to be enjoyed also. Sit in your solitude, be it on balcony or in a back garden or by a window box. All nature is beautiful;

some just waits to be noticed more than others. Let the sun on your face, feel the warmth on your shoulders. Paddle in the water or just sit on a rock and watch the water flow. If you can get to it sink your feet into some warm sand and smell the sea. The spring is fresh and clean and refreshing. This is the time to engage in all the outdoor pursuits you have been planning all winter. Whether it is exercises or socialising or entertainment or all three just get out there and enjoy. Put away your socks drag out your sandals. Throw open your windows, listen to the birds at dawn. It is almost the summer, be glad and rejoice because remember that our seasons can pass quickly and need to be enjoyed fairly instantly.

~

April 4th

On being a woman/mother

It is as much of a real dilemma today as it was years ago. We are encouraged to have careers and then face glass ceilings. We are motivated to wait to have our children and then are told we are old having them. We are encouraged to work and then told to stay at home. We are always torn because we do not want children/do not have children/cannot have children/have children and must put up with all society have to say about that.

The very people advising us commonly or should I say telling us what to do didn't themselves and won't make the choices required. We must be strong. We must ignore fashions. We must do what feels right for us at the time. This will be right for our families. We must distance ourselves from what others think or we will never be happy. There are no rights or wrongs in this. Each of us is unique and what is right for one is not for another. Being a female is a constant contradiction between a woman's career and home and the balance is the hardest act to achieve. There is no guilt. This is just the way life is. Use your information to hand and make your decision. Your decision whatever it is, if it feels right then it is for the best. Follow your gut instinct and you will not go wrong.

~

April 5th

Roots-Identity

Knowing where you come from really helps with finding out who you are. It is very hard to go forward in life unless you know where you came from. If you are in foster care or adopted or whatever your circumstances knowing how you came to be can influence how you see yourself and how you go forward in life. In the big picture identifying with your roots and your culture plays an important role. Whatever nationality you are I am sure you are proud of it. If like me you are Irish, well apart from all the potatoes! I am proud of our music both traditional and contemporary, of the fact we all have a book in us (even if some only express it in the pub!), I am proud of our smile, our hard work and our craic. I love being Irish and would hate to be anything else. Wherever you hail from I bet it is the same for you. And so it should be. As you journey to understand who you are and where you want to go, listen to the roots of your land. Enjoy the music, poetry, movies, food, sport or whatever your country is famous for. Revel in the pride and the glory of your home-place, and then take those seeds with you as you plant your new world.

~

April 6th

You must do your thing

You must do that thing-you think you cannot do. We all feel like this at one time or another. There is a big road block and we do not know what to do about it. It's like a big blockage in our heads. We cannot go through it so we try to go around it but we cannot. Maybe we can climb over it. Everything, to most of us, seems huge at first but can in fact be broken down into a series of manageable tasks.

Most situations have a solution it is just that it is often quite different than what we envisage and can be hard to see. Whatever weighs on your mind, try looking at it in novel ways. Face it and look at it dead in the eye. The thing that you think that you cannot do is often the thing you must overcome. Imagine you what succeeding in it and overcoming it. Feel the glorious after effects of it and the joyous result. Break down the problem into sections and plan to achieve each one bit by bit. Nothing is fully blocked and when you hit a block look around for other solutions. Tell yourself that you believe in yourself. Know that you can do it. When you know that you can you are far more likely to succeed. This is better than putting you down. Finally every step of the way reward yourself for all that you have accomplished and recognise it. The journey is long and the reward, though worth it, may often feel short lived. When you break down the journey you can enjoy each tiny little step, and in the end reward yourself for a job well done.

~

April 7th

Follow your heart

Follow your heart-It will rarely see you wrong. Ever been in a shop or at a sale of work and have you ever seen something and just been drawn to it.

It is like you are connected to it in some way or another. For just one euro what harm will it do and so home it comes with you. Sometimes I buy objects not really knowing why and then they can end up being the perfect gift for someone a week or two later or something someone in the family needs out of the blue. More personally I was once asked out on a date and whilst my brain was dubious my heart said yes. I never looked back. It was a wonderful decision that if I had listened to my brain I may not have made. The heart on many levels gives out messages if only we would listen. Often we ask questions when we know in our heart and soul what the true answers are. We are just not always ready to face it yet. So we keep searching outside of ourselves. A feeling in your heart is very genuine. Your heart does not have an ego and is not trying to impress anyone. Your heart is part of your quiet voice within. So whether it is for something big or something small, follow your heart it will always bring you home happy.

~

April 8th

Easter

In our house Easter is a bit like a mini Christmas. Even though this year it does not fall for another two weeks, it is no harm to start thinking in advance about it. There are the ceremonies, the gifts and the compulsory nosh up. The children run around our home and garden searching frantically for eggs which hopefully have not been snapped up by our feathered friends. (That actually happened last year!) Celebrations of any kind are a great excuse to bring everyone together. Be they friends, family or new acquaintances. It is good to take advantage of these times to unwind and enjoy the company of those you may not see every day. To catch up if you have a little extra time, as life can move very fast and sometimes it can seem like there is no time. Consider a barbecue or a dinner party or even just a coffee with those you care about. Festive times, bank holidays can be lonely times for some so why not see it as a great chance for others or you to enjoy a well- earned change of scenery or just a catch-up.

~

April 9th

At a low ebb

If you are at a low ebb and not really feeling able for much around now then that's when everything looks different. When you are happy and someone makes inappropriate or unpleasant comments you can generally let it go however when you are a little down you feel vulnerable and it hits you hard.

Even though you already know this and it is not rational it can still often really get to you. These are the days to be especially good to you. People who upset you in whatever way are not thinking about you and are living in their own separate world. They do not realise the pain they are causing you. If you have your basics to do then do them but nothing extra save to make your world safe, comfortable, serene and warm for you. This is what you deserve, so mind yourself. Everything passes eventually and if you just let it be, the chances are that tomorrow you will feel much better. For me it is a warm bath, a snugly bathrobe, and soft music. For others it can be a good book, a brisk walk. Do whatever works for you. Accept that we all have down days. Know that its normal and that it will improve and everything will seem much brighter very soon.

~

April 10th

A tiny thoughtful deed

Today do a thoughtful deed that will surprise someone. It is even better if they do not know where it came from. Enjoy how good it feels to do something good even if it is only a small thing. People generally remember thoughtful actions and they are so happy that you took the time to think of them. What deed you do is not important. It could be anything from paying the next guys toll on the motor-way to opening a door for a stressed mother. Doing something that helps to ease the burden of another spontaneously. Big fancy gestures are nice and fun to do, yet it is the thoughtful ones that you will be remembered for even if they don't know your name. That time you made a mixed playlist to cheer up a friend or baked a cake or knitted a jumper or washed their dog. So get thinking and do something, anything that will make someone else feel better. You will be amazed at the joy you bring and astounded at the joy you receive.

~

April 11th

Judgmental

I was watching one of those afternoon talk shows and it was all about your home. The presenter believed that every room should be presentable and whatever room was not was a poor reflection on your state of mind in that area. Well I watched the show and I watched as we were led through her home, an exclusive New York apartment with a walk in wardrobe, with an entire room of clothing and shoes, it quite resembled a shop. Everything was neatly arranged on shelves and it was massive. I was very disheartened initially by this on two counts. Firstly, I longed to see a programme of this kind showing an ordinary house or flat where someone has made an effort. I really felt that I could not relate to this home at all. Secondly, the idea that just because I have a porch that mostly needs to be replaced does not make me a miserable person. I felt misjudged. I and most of us would have amazing homes if we could only afford it and being lectured on this by someone excessively rich or someone with a gigantic cash flow is very annoying. Then I got to thinking. I looked around my home. Yes, there were a lot of mistakes and it was true that the first impression of a home lasts so I tried to be a little less judgmental and set about fixing my home. Now without cleaners or much cash I have removed lots of objects that I will never miss including furniture leaflets and bills. It still looks less than presentable for television but I feel that I am getting there and at least when it is finally finished all of us who live here shall know that this home is ours and reflects us and no one else. I do not mind being judged on that.

~

April 12th

Culture

In my culture when it is your birthday no matter what age you are, out come candles, a cake, and the happy birthday song often followed by three hurrahs. It could be at home, in a restaurant, pub or even in your office. We all kind of cringe when it is our turn but in another way we know it is as it should be. Then you make a wish and blow out your candles. If you blow out all your candles together your wish comes true. I have been blowing away on and off for many years. There have been many situations, many homes, with varied circumstances. I have gone from excited to hating it, to cynical boredom, to being proud that I am still here to do it. Now I register it is a great tradition. The singing can be appalling, the cakes varied but the unity and the thought that goes with it is priceless. You can get new traditions in your culture any time you wish. This year I started an Easter egg hunt and announced it as a tradition. It is that easy. So what would you like? Sit down dinner together once a week; breakfast in bed every Saturday or just on your birthday? Whatever customs you want they are yours to make. The people in your life will learn to love them even if at first they say they do not. If you sail alone, then better again, you can really indulge your ideas and set up many self-nurturing traditions to build up your resource. Along with the seasons traditions are a lovely framework that provide us with a road map to follow on our journey through life.

~

April 13th

The 18 40 60 rule

You may have already heard about this rule before; however it is worth mentioning as it is very interesting and strangely true to most of us. At eighteen all you really care about is what people are thinking about you. At forty you really no longer care what they think of you. At sixty you notice most people couldn't care less and are far too busy thinking about themselves! Simple but true. I am in my late thirties and I have just become aware that the world is in fact NOT preoccupied with my existence. It is such a relief to find that out and that when we feel we are maybe being ignored the fact is that people are busy with their own lives and rightly so. The fact that every decision we make mostly does not mean a hill of beans to others unless it affects them means in turn that you develop a freer existence. Not worrying about what you imagine others are thinking about you leaves you free to make the choices you know are right- without fear or favour.

~

April 14th

Quality

So you have started making new choices and recognising the old ones and are worried about what this new quality of life will cost you. You may have chosen to eat better food, better bread with less sugar but twice the price. You imagine it will cripple you financially if you allow this new thinking to infiltrate your life. The reverse however is actually true. The better you treat yourself, the more self-worth you have. The more self-worth you have the better your quality of life. The better your quality of life the happier you are so the better you treat yourself. It becomes a circle of success. Quality is always better than quantity. One good shirt that sits well and washes well in a classic colour, well cut, always stands the test of time. Quality is a choice and not a treat. Remember that. You are worth it, so choose quality. We all know the difference between quality and paying for exclusive brand names and we all know the genuine article when we see it so do not be misled by flashy outlets that are overpriced. Their lights will dim all too quickly. Remember who you are. Keep in mind what you want. Remember quality is just what you deserve.

~

April 15th

Mingling

You know how it goes, there are phases in your life where you are always going out and phases were you rarely go out and then times where you go out maybe every other week.

Well recently I have been to various functions including a 21st, 50th and a housewarming (This makes me sound quite popular but really it is just a rare run!) and have met many and varied people.

It is only when you break out of your standard circle and your routine (be it family, work colleagues or friends) that you perceive that other people in other worlds exist at all. You hear about them, maybe see them on television but there is nothing like being thrown into a room full of strangers, to surprisingly concentrate the mind.

Today, I attended a housewarming of an old school friend with whom I had barely kept in touch. It was fabulous to meet some new people, some people I already knew and so refreshing to interact in a new environment.

The most exhilarating persons that I met tonight at thirty eight years old had had many careers and roles yet they were still so enthused about life. Some were searching for that job, man, home or life experience. They were like a breath of fresh air. Some had been lucky and found what they wanted while young or accepted what they had and didn't ponder it too much.

Some however talked quickly with arms waving and big lit up eyes about what they wanted out of life. These are exciting people to be around as their genuine appreciation of life is infectious.

~

April 16th

Choice

First you need to look at the life and lifestyle you have and the choices you have made. You might not see the choices straight away and you might think that you have made none. Still everything is a choice. The job you are in or not in, you chose to be there. They may have chosen you from a line of applicants but you applied and you accepted.

The flat, bedsit or house or bedroom you live in was chosen and accepted by you. You set a place in your head below which you would not accept. Then you accepted what you achieved. Or put it another way you achieved what you expected. If you wanted a fancier place to live in you would have kept looking until you reached your yardstick. You had a choice.

Exactly where you are right now in your life is your choice. You are destined to make choices if you want to change anything. The trick is to begin to realise when you are making these. Become aware of what is going on in your life. Do you buy a lovely throw for your couch that matches the room or anything to hide a stain? Do you buy quality material that will last or an average one the wrong shade because it is inexpensive but will not wash well? Know this about yourself and go to work there. Accept and own your decisions. Be aware that you always have a choice and exercise your right to choose.

One other thing, I hear some saying you can't afford it and that I do understand. Well, better to wait six months and get one lovely comfortable pair of shoes that will last five years, than five cheap throwaway ones or ones you do not really love. Watch the sales in the pricey places, there is always a trend. Make your choices and accept them.

~

April 17th

What you cannot do

Every-day there is something we do not get to because we think we cannot do it. It may be something simple like leaving work on time, to the complexities of finishing the crossword but whatever it is, its weight can feel very heavy. Carrying this, daily, can be exhausting mentally. Sometimes I become annoyed with myself for not doing it and put it off then time runs out.

What if you did your most difficult task first? If you decide to do one awkward thing and do it early on in the day it can be a great relief. I find even making a paper list of chores helps and crossing them off as you go.

You will feel so proud of yourself, your world will seem much lighter and you will be happier if you can just get rid of one annoying chore. Your self-worth will be better knowing what you have accomplished and how hard it was for you. It may be something as simple as taking time to eat a healthy breakfast or doing a few push-ups, whatever niggles in your head get it out. Otherwise it will hold you back. This can then get in the way of other vital things that you need to do.

~

April 18th

A VIP Dinner

You know that time when you had someone special over for a meal. You cleaned everything. You laid an impeccable table, you brought fresh flowers, manicured your nails. Well maybe you haven't done it yet but if you did you know what you would do.

Well now is your chance. Prepare fresh decent produce prepared earlier that day for the special guest who is visiting you on the evening of your choice. Get the crystal out or at least abandon the kids glasses! Fold your best napkins and choose apt music. Guess who is coming to dinner? It is the most important person in your life. You of course!

There is only one YOU which makes you very special. We rarely treat ourselves and when eating alone tend to stint on presentation and atmosphere.

I challenge you to put on a tremendous night for yourself with all the trimmings and to truly enjoy it with not one ounce of guilt. You deserve it! You owe it to yourself. In this dinner you not only get to be the hostess you also get to be the VIP!

~

April 19th

Flexibility

Apart from being true to you a person needs to also be flexible. If something is not going to work one way there is always another. That is the beauty of life. Look at all the ways children move about before they walk. Some cruise, some shuffle, some roll, some creep but in the end, mostly, they all walk. There is no right way there is just the way that works for them. So let your mind wander and see what way it thinks you should go. That is probably the right way. Trust your instincts. Be open to being flexible. Be willing to change a plan that is not working. And remember a ruler is flexible but it never breaks.

~

April 20th

Practice, practice, practice

You know that if you want to be an amazing Pianist or Violinist or Singer or whatever then you must practice. Well turning your life around is not all that different. Whatever you are changing or adjusting in your life it will require practice. Now I do not necessarily mean practice driving that new car (though that's no bad idea either!) I mean live and re-live the moment of your final achievement in your mind wherever and whenever you can, even if it seems silly.

When the time comes to do it for real you will be more than ready. If you particularly imagine something in your head at bus stops, sandwich queues and bank queues it will eventually get into your subconscious. If you have time and a sense of humour and a bit of a nerve act it out as if it is happening maybe with someone you trust- it will be good fun and you will probably laugh a lot too.

If your ambition is simply time to yourself then practice that in your mind. See yourself in your ideal spot doing what you love best, your home at peace and see you feeling relaxed. If your dream is a law degree imagine your graduation day. Never underestimate the power of your mind and its ability to get the results that you dream of. Every scene you present to your mind, your mind works hard to make it real for you. So Practice, practice, practice I promise it will be worth it.

~

April 21st

Appreciating our lives

At some time in our lives most of us will experience an illness or circumstances that are fairly serious. When this happens we will worry less about the trivial thoughts that mostly perturb us now. We will appreciate our family, our home, the richness of our lives but if only we could appreciate them all the time.

Our lives then will seem so much sunnier as we compare them to the truly serious situation that we are presented with. Now the fact that we know this right now shows that somewhere deep down we know we have lovely aspects to our lives. So why not appreciate them right here and right now. Why wait until something serious or near fatal occurs?

Anything can happen in life. We will not live forever; we may not always be able to do what we can right here and now. So we should be grateful for what we have and instead of worrying over whatever may happen we should take great joy in the lives we have, the roof over our heads (no matter how simple), the bread on our table and the love that surrounds us.

Once we do this then we will find a staggering increase in the joy in our lives. Taking a little time each day to appreciate all we have will enrich our lives vastly and help us to really value tem.

~

April 22nd

Are you ready?

Is it all too much? Do you not feel ready yet for any change? Maybe you are happy enough in your present situation complaining about something to yourself with no real solution in your mind. Lots of people are much happier with what they know rather than the unknown even if they do not like what they know all that much.

We tend to feel safe and secure because we think we know what to expect even though in truth we rarely do. It really makes no difference. Things happen all the time to shake up our world. We may as well be the author of a few of them.

Isn't it better to have had a go then at whatever it is that you really want rather than to grow old wondering what if you had acted on it? I promised myself early on in life I would never be a "what iffer" the result has produced many situations, not all of then successful, but at least I will always know how I tried. I had a go and gave circumstances my best shot.

So think today, if you are not ready for a big change then make a little one to start, have one less sugar in your tea, eat one less biscuit, taking a ten minute walk. Whatever you choose it is a start and when you feel you are truly ready, your body and mind will be ready too. And anyway those entire tiny little baby steps are always often silently bringing you closer to what you want.

~

April 23rd

Watch the signal

We all have things that start the cycle that stresses us out. The key in managing our stress is to know and spot what stresses us out sometime when we are relaxed. Then we can learn to either avoid that situation where possible or prepare for it in advance if we feel it is inevitable.

Maybe it is just a certain gesture your boss uses or a comment issued by a loved one that really gets on your nerves. Well know this, people that really hurt you like this do not notice what they are actually doing. They are in their own world and certainly don't mean you any particular harm.

Pick a happy relaxed day and gently mention how upset you were about the comment/statement and ask them nicely to find a new method of expressing how they feel. Or better still, to communicate earlier on so that there is no need for any stressful comments.

I guarantee you that they will not be even aware of the stress you are experiencing. It seems big to you because it is happening to you however to others it is just a little thing. So plan to relieve your stress before it gets too big and gets in the way of you enjoying your life.

~

April 24th

Help-everyone needs it

Even or especially the seemingly strong people in life all need help at one time or another. So do not be too embarrassed to ask for help when you positively need it. It takes a much bigger person to ask for help than a person who buckles under the strain or gives up.

In a career situation people will mostly be flattered if you ask their advice. Take one to lunch ask the questions and note their answers. If you badly need a decent baby sitter ask a family member or a good friend- someone will know someone. If want to take a night class ring in for the leaflets. You get the picture. Whatever you need or need to know never be afraid to search for it. Get books from the library, see how others did it. Most things have been done in some form by someone. Use their experiences to help your idea take form. Trying the www is good too. However, there is nothing like talking to people who have walked a similar road. They can help with potholes and pitfalls by spotting them even before you know they are there.

~

April 25th

Time out

Every so often even if it is only once a year we all need a time out day. Get up normally, see the family off or if alone have breakfast as usual then at the time when you normally do something STOP. Stop and take a really big time out.

Play some nice music, maybe run a luxurious bath and read, or sit outside or sort out your favourite possessions. So long as it is a relaxing pursuit, do it. Turn off the phone, computer and mobile phone. Treat yourself as you would a relation who is poorly. Be really kind to yourself. Don't feel bad. We all need a day off every once in a while to just relax and re-group and this is yours, enjoy it.

~

April 26th

Testing

They have an arrangement in an Irish car company where in the summer months you can test drive a car for three days. Normal test drives are half an hour with the salesman by your side-it is very difficult to get a real feel for the car under these conditions, so three days is just perfect.

So, what would you like to test? A new look in you or in your home? Try out altered combinations in your appearance and see what you think. You can do this in your own environment far from prying eyes. If you are really self- conscious hide in the bathroom! When you get one you might like test drive it for a few days and see how it makes you feel as a person and what reactions you get from others.

Do people treat you in a different way because you look different? Do you like it? Listen to the positive criticism and let the negative go. Have fun discussing who you want to be. Who you really are, costs nothing.

Then go to work on your home. Put a throw on the couch. If you hate it, remove it. Change your pictures around. Re-arrange the furniture. How does it feel? Maybe buy new pretty cushion covers and pop them on. Such a simple thing can really transform a space and how you feel about it.

Have fun. Test everything. Pass what suits and release what you no longer need. The world can be testing for you, so test your world for yourself!

~

April 27th

A change of scenery

If like me you spend a large part of your day inside then in the evenings you often feel you need a change of scenery. If you are not blessed with a garden to maintain then find yourself a nice park bench. Sitting for a little while as evening is closing in watching the birds go about their business and the cats go after them can be very relaxing. As you sit there you realise the outdoor world turns continuously whether you close that deal or polish that table, or not.

The simplicity of nature is very soothing. It can be like a piece of music watching birds building their nests and foraging for food, the sun setting here and rising somewhere else. As you sit there you observe the beauty and perfection of it all as it seeps into your being, you understand your part though significant in the world is very small and what keeps you awake at night worrying will not stop the sun setting tonight or rising tomorrow.

So after your day is done, sit down, take off your shoes, feel the earth beneath your feet and relax.

~

April 28th

Follow your instincts

Any time is good for a Barbie!!!

It is the May bank holiday weekend here and with an air of optimism known only to the Irish, with our consistently unpredictable weather, we drag out our outdoor furniture clean up our barbeque and purchase the produce.

The day starts fine yet breezy 15 degrees Celsius, then a little cooler, then a few drops of rain by 6.30pm official kick off time the heavens have opened and the rains have come. Our barbeque is however burning brightly alongside a large patio heater and the chef is cooking merrily seemingly oblivious to the rain.

The guests tucked up indoors slip out periodically to be polite and inhale the smoke and grab a bit of atmosphere in other words get wet!

Believe it or not as our first barbeque, notwithstanding the weather, it was a great success. The flavour of the food was lovely and the company was great. To the outside eye it would have looked like a disaster. We could have let the rain frighten us off but we stuck to our guns and had a super evening. Follow your instincts. Do what feels right for you-even if you get very wet and everyone thinks you are nuts!

~

April 29th

Where is the fire?

There are so many stressed people in the world and we suffer so much anxiety in our lives some of which is so needless. Those who keep a home notably often feel as if it is all going wrong when the floor is dirty or the kitchen is a mess. They feel they are fighting a losing battle to sustain a high standard and yet the battle rages on. In actual fact there is no emergency at all, only in our own heads. We can end up at therapists, doctors and feel very down in our attempts to maintain levels of life that are totally unnecessary. There is no emergency in reality. Everything will never be perfect. The closer we get to excellence the more we notice more to be changed, fixed or improved. It is a continuous journey. Even if we consider we have reached the finish line it will seem like time to start again, maybe redecorate.

So do not panic about objects not being perfect around you. Life will go on just the same without hotel quality or style and the more you release the control on having everything perfect the more you can enjoy life and the company of those around you. This is much more relaxing and fun and what life is actually about.

~

April 30th

On skips and clutter

You can imagine what I think about skips. Dirty smelly stinking skips. I love them. There is nothing like seeing one arrive and nothing like seeing it leave.

A skip is symbolic of everything. We lose all the old worn out junk and make new space. Even as the skip was being filled up we both turned to each other and said "Things are starting to take shape in the garden". Clutter hides so much beauty. We had so much disorder until very recently, old bikes, bits of wood, bits of cars, old machines. I like to imagine that we are all much the same with clutter.

If you have a second hand home and renovate and make it your own then you end up with a lot of leftovers. When you can mentally face it the best thing to do is to de clutter. You will be amazed how relieved you feel when it's all gone and your home looks so much better and bigger. You then have the chance to put your stamp on it and make it pretty.

A skip is of course rather a drastic step. Firstly I would suggest a bag and toss in old brochures and pamphlets for recycling. Ease yourself into the de clutter as it can be rather emotional. Some of us feel safer to be surrounded by a lot of stuff, even if it personally does not mean much to us. When we see the space clearing we can feel a little vulnerable and fragile. But do not worry you soon get used to the new arrangement and miss almost none of it.

So, maybe today you will sort your sock drawer and throw out the odd ones. Recycle the old newspapers and packaging. Start small, do a little each day. See how good it feels.

In a few days you will feel a genuine lift and an enormous sense of achievement.

~

As we draw to a close on this season here below are some of the ideas from April to ponder on. I have included some note pages at the back of this book for you to add your own notes and make plans. Life has a way of getting in the way of our pursuits so at least if we write them down we are one step closer to success.

- Follow your heart
- Build traditions
- Test drive ideas
- Expect quality
- Strive for flexibility
- Follow deep appreciation
- Practice, Practice, Practice

My notes for February

My notes for March

My notes for April

AFTERWORD

This book is dedicated to my second son Aaron.

With many thanks to all those who have supported me in making this possible including a great deal of gratitude to my Dad Tony who helped with editing it and gently noting subtle changes that needed to be made. My family for giving me the space to write night after night in my water bed as the babies slept. My big brother Fin who constantly encouraged me and last but not least my husband Tony without whom little would have happened. His never ending support and love has taken me through the worst storms and his wise words ring out in my head "Keep it simple, sexy". Thank you so much for everything.

11 November 2013

Sheila Keegan Groome loves life and lives it with a real passion. This is her first book in a series of four taking you through the year season by season and day by day. Simply be-Summer is due out later in 2014.

She lives in Ireland with her husband Tony and has four children Seán, Aaron, Oisín and Mary.

You can visit Sheila at simplybesheilakeegan.wordpress.com and purchase additional copies of her books in all major bookshops and on the internet.